A MYSTERIOUS HUMMING NOISE

OTHER BOOKS BY HOWARD WHITE

POETRY

The Men There Were Then

Ghost in the Gears

NON-FICTION

A Hard Man to Beat

The Sunshine Coast

HUMOUR

Writing in the Rain

CHILDREN'S

Patrick and the Backhoe

The Airplane Ride

A Mysterious Humming Noise

NEW POEMS BY
HOWARD WHITE

ANVIL PRESS / VANCOUVER

Copyright © 2019 by Howard White

All rights reserved. No part of this book may be reproduced by any means
without the prior written permission of the publisher, with the exception of
brief passages in reviews. Any request for photocopying or other repro-
graphic copying of any part of this book must be directed in writing to Access
Copyright: The Canadian Copyright Licensing Agency, One Yonge Street,
Suite 800, Toronto, Ontario, Canada, M5E 1E5.

Anvil Press Publishers Inc.
P.O. Box 3008, Main Post Office
Vancouver, B.C. V6B 3X5 Canada
www.anvilpress.com

Library and Archives Canada Cataloguing in Publication
Title: A mysterious humming noise / poetry by Howard White.
Names: White, Howard, 1945- author.
Identifiers: Canadiana 20190088753 | ISBN 9781772141412 (softcover)
Classification: LCC PS8595.H4186 M97 2019 | DDC C811/.54—dc23

Cover design by Derek von Essen
Interior by HeimatHouse
Author photo by Brian Lee
Represented in Canada by Publishers Group Canada
Distributed by Raincoast Books

The publisher gratefully acknowledges the financial assistance of the Canada
Council for the Arts, the Canada Book Fund, and the Province of British
Columbia through the B.C. Arts Council and the Book Publishing Tax Credit.

PRINTED AND BOUND IN CANADA

For Simone, Eloise, Callan and Ian White

TABLE OF CONTENTS

1. THAT FIZZY FEELING

The Repairman / 13

What I Learned Bulldozing / 15

Explanation / 18

All My Friends I Don't Have / 20

Sand / 21

Baseball / 23

That Fizzy Feeling / 26

My To-Do List / 28

Technique / 29

Romancing the Gnome / 31

Street Dance / 32

January 1, 2016 / 34

Nature Facts / 36

Sympathy / 38

2. MUNGA

The Old Man Plans His Memoir / 43

Munga's Methods / 45

Oldtimer / 47

Faulty Assumptions / 48

Munga's Final Thoughts on the Matter / 49

Denouement / 53

Escapism / 55

Not Shooting Pop / 56

3. TWO WAYS TO BE BRILLIANT

Wharves / 59

Parents / 60

The Secret of the Pyramids / 61

Free Tickets to Ron Sexsmith / 63

Love / 65

Raccoon Pass / 66

Ode to A Stump / 68

No Ordinary Bill / 70

On the Passing of Captain Upfuck / 74

To A Urologist / 76

Two Ways to Be Brilliant / 77

Agamemnon / 78

Coition / 80

At the Coffee Machine / 81

Toxins / 82

News from Space / 83

The Sea Otter / 84

4. WHEN I HAD A GARDEN

The Book of Earth / 89

Apology to Alfred Page / 90

Brainfarts / 91

Woodpile / 93

Retrieval / 94

Relativity / 95

Old Folks at Home / 96

Dementia / 97

5. THE CONSTANT URGE

My Influences / 101

Faster Than a Speeding Bullet / 102

Three / 103

Sample / 104

Poets on Themselves / 105

Death of a Poet / 106

Fandom / 107

Talking About It / 108

Enough About the Moon / 109

Mrs. Fleming / 110

Accidental Chronicler / 112

Tough Bug / 114

Poetry / 115

Acknowledgements / 117

About the Author / 118

1.

THAT FIZZY FEELING

THE REPAIRMAN

Fall is here, it can't be denied
The pounding rains arouse in me a shapeless menace
As I picture the leaf-clogged eavestroughs, the skimpy woodpile
And the things I discovered wrong with the boat
On our last trip of the summer
The mysterious electrical leak that flatted the battery
The equally mysterious accumulation of water
Along one side of the bilge only
Not to mention several things I have known about for years
Like the deteriorating floor. This is just the boat.
Elsewhere my life seems equally unready for winter
And I fret about it, wondering what to do—
Call in help? What kind of help and where do you go?
We are not a family that ever called the repairman
My father always fixed the electric stove himself
Sometimes showering us with sparks
And leaving it with one burner feeble
But mostly leaving things on his job list unreached
This is the approach I inherit and many hundreds of hours
Have I worried and wondered about that roof leak
Which I patched and re-patched to no effect
Until finally I broke down and got a roofer to look at
He found the problem in about three minutes
Laughed at my befuddlement, sticking his fat pencil
Down the hole for emphasis, didn't charge for the callout
But told me I needed a new roof anyway, for about $10,000
Now here is my dilemma: do I call in the repairman
For everything? My out-of-control waistline?
My aching joints? My poor family relations?

/ 13

My overloaded in-basket? My faulty memory?
There are no doubt repairmen for all these malfunctions
Listed in the online yellow pages awaiting my call
Where do you draw the line between
Trying to manage things yourself
And turning your life entirely over to qualified professionals?
I pick up my dad's old screwdriver and move
Toward the electric range, which has been
Making a mysterious humming noise

WHAT I LEARNED BULLDOZING

I learned to look for the water.
Every site, at least in the temperate zone, has water running
    through it.
If you bite into it with your bulldozer blade, you will disrupt its flow.
It will pool around the machine and turn the soil to soup you
    can't work.
So your first move must be to figure out where the water's coming
    from and going to
And route it around your work. Obvious when you see it at last
But it took me several years of wallowing in mud.

Another thing was to judge the material.
Sticky clay or grainy sand? Soupy loonshit or iron hardpan?
On one of my first jobs up north I spent all day wallowing in loonshit
So formless you couldn't get traction or make it stay put.
The foreman, a wag named Fred, said, "Hey, just make it flat.
Forget about the fancy wavy stuff."
I told him how impossible it was to do anything with that muck.
"It's not that deep is it?" he said. "Just get rid of it."
I assured him it was bottomless, a Marianas of mud.
"Here, let me have a go at that, I think you can get under it."
So I climbed off and he throttled up and bit down into the miasma,
Spinning out and wallowing, deeper than I had dared dig.
The cat's powerful tracks reduced to spinning uselessness
Until suddenly they bit something solid and the motor lugged down,
The dozer's deadly force restored, and he began ploughing great
    bladefuls
Over the edge, revealing a subcutaneous stratum of dry workable
    dirt.

He jumped off with a grin, saying "Hell that muck is just sittin' on top.
Just sluice it all out of your way and you'll be fine."
"How in hell did you know the mud was only three feet deep?"
I asked, incredulous and humiliated.
"You can't make a hole in soup no matter how many times you poke it,"
He explained. "If you find yourself doing something over and over
And it's not working over and over, well you either have to give up or
    do something different. And there is always something different, if
    you just figure what it is. You'll learn."
So many times since, when mired down in taxes and regulations,
I've found my way by asking, "I wonder how deep this loonshit is?"

Finally, there was the sandbox. That one came to me at Revelstoke.
It was my first big job, where I was completely on my own
With no sympathetic Fred to guide me.
They dumped me in the middle of a cottonwood forest and told me—
    well, nothing
Except I could see they were clearing the valley for a reservoir.
I was completely lost at first, not knowing where or how to start
And plunged around making a mess for half a day
Knowing I was once again poking holes in soup but not knowing what
    else to do.
It was all so strange and high-pressure and complicated.
So I stopped and climbed up on top of the D8's cab to look around
And that is when I invoked my childhood sandbox.
"Now, if I was five again and playing in my sandbox, what would I do?"
Looking through that lens of simplification, my course was clear
And I set busily to work, imagining the blade was a Tonka toy in my hand
Instead of a dozer attached to a huge roaring crawler tractor.
When the foreman came around to check he said, "A little rough,
But I can see you've got the idea. Just keep working like you are."

How many times since then, beset by financial wolves
And tossed on emotional seas with no landmark in sight,
I've invoked my sandbox vision, imagined the boy with his toy
And the slightly bigger boy with his Revelstoke bulldozer
And all confusion drops away.

EXPLANATION

If you want to get something done, get a logger
—BC coast saying

My father was a logger.
He taught me to rush in where angels fear to tread
And move that wood.
We loggers have no time for ceremony.
We think only in broad strokes.
Though I have spent most of my life shuffling paper
My dad's old logger ethic has served me well.
It has let me take on challenges
I was totally unqualified for
Like publishing books
And successfully publish 968 of the suckers.
People who worked with me say
The one most valuable thing they learned from me
Was not to get all your ducks in a row
But to plunge in and just do it.
But in the true spirit of the grass is always greener etc
I give myself very little credit for this
And instead envy those who can do fine cabinetry
Printers who can get everything set just right
So the whole run goes through without a hitch.
I built a print shop and overhauled a big offset press
But could never manage to get through a job
Without making the type too blobby or too thin
And spoiling acres of paper.
Even though I was doing everything you were supposed to do
I just wasn't getting the adjustments fine enough.

That was beyond me.
Using my broad strokes approach I can make anything work
Without reading the instruction book.
I just size it up—there's the intake, there's the exhaust
And that green button will be the starter:
Fire in the hole!
I will have the job finished while the other guy is still watching the tutorial.
But the machine's inner nature will remain a mystery to me.
My nephews all took science and had a science teacher for a father
And they always know inner designs of things:
Why I always get unwanted frames around my text
And where to look to turn that feature off.
They have a habit of mind of asking why and how
A thing does what it does
Where I just settle for knowing it does it.
This often gets me very down on myself
Thinking I have kind of faked my way through this life
And never really learned or truly understood a goddamn thing.
That's when it helps to do a vanity Google,
Count those books
And take comfort
In the sheer volume of my folly.

ALL MY FRIENDS I DON'T HAVE

I had actually planned to have a lot more friends than this.
I have hardly any—in fact only one real everyday one
Who is unfortunately kind of ridiculous as a person.
Luckily she never reads poetry so I can say that.
A lot of people have sort of showed up on my computer screen
Offering friendship and I guess they have wandered off feeling rejected
And probably resentful, thinking I am an arrogant, self-absorbed prick.
I am sure Mac Allison thinks that, and Barry Edwardson,
Two old friends who reached out and visited me and asked me to come
    to visit them
But I never did. Now one of my last pairs of friends,
Allan and Inge, seem to have gone cool.
This is mostly because of neglect I think.
Or maybe a bit because I'm sort of angry and negative all the time.
They are lovers of everybody and believers in the great middleclass myth
That all is for the best and all will work out in the end
Which I admittedly have run out of patience with. If I ever had any.
But friends will overlook that if you pay attention to them.
That is my most characteristic failing:
I just never call, never go visit, never reciprocate.
I put this down to being busy and consumed with work.
Other people can be much busier than me and still have big social lives
But I am a single-focus guy, and also a guy who thinks work comes first
By several miles over any lightweight stuff.
The nice thing probably about this is that it is curable, if I am curable.
If I reached back out to Mac and Barry and the Dixons
I am sure they would warm up.
But already I am thinking, aw fuck it.

SAND

Max Andersen and I have a long-running argument about sand.
It got started way back in the early seventies when I wrote something
About the quality of sand to be found at Cape Caution
Where I had never been but had visited in my mind
Finding it a desolate, windswept place exposed
To the fiercest storms of the open Pacific
Where the sand had been ground fine as dust:
Bluish-tinged dust as I imagined it, perhaps
Thinking of the rock dust made by jackhammers.
Max, who had never been there either, took issue
Saying sand doesn't work like that.
It doesn't keep getting infinitely finer
Because it reaches a point where the grains are so small
When they bang on each other they don't break anymore
They're so light they just bounce off each other harmlessly.
Max was an endlessly subtle thinker not to say an engineer
And his keen analysis was a match for my legendary stubbornness
As the two forces ground upon each other over the glacial decades
Reducing the points for and against to a fine bluish dust
That we nevertheless take up with fresh determination
Upon our increasingly rare encounters (he lives in Mexico now).

I would like to show Max this manuscript that just came in
From the retired head of the Geological Survey of Canada
A PhD and FRCS who has made a life study of sand
And now wants me to publish a 1000-page book about it.
He has microscopic photos of grains of all the different kinds of sand:
Black Arabian sand made from obsidian, white atoll sand made from coral,

/ 21

Coarse young sand made from seashells and sand made from good
    old granite
Such as the sand at Cape Caution, which turns out to be brown,
    not blue.
But not even he could not put an end to the glacial grinding of
    our debate,
Saying that while the erosive process would diminish as the mass
Of Cape Caution's sand grains declined, this could be counteracted
By the elevated energy input of the open Pacific, meaning that while
The smallening of the sand grains would slow exponentially
It would never cease entirely.
Max and I both claimed victory at this news
He saying once the grains had reached the usual size
The smallification process would have slowed to such a crawl
It would have for all intents and purposes stopped
Leaving the sand at Cape Caution completely normal looking.
I said, no, in geological time forever is nothing
And these sands had all the time they needed to become quite floury.
To which Max said no, this is a relatively new beach
In place only since the last ice-age, a mere instant in geologic time.

We started this argument when we were in our early twenties
And I am now seventy so I don't know how much smaller
We can grind our points before we ourselves attain infinity.

BASEBALL

I owe a lot to baseball. I never saw a baseball until I was 12.
We called it a hardball, to distinguish it from the more common
Ball we played with at school, the softball.
Baseball was something learned outside school,
A civilian pursuit run by men of the town
And way more serious than school games of scrub.
I remember Gordie Gough opining a hardball could kill ya.
I didn't know any better than to try out for the
Little League team, figuring I had learned enough at school
To overcome my years of ball-less home schooling
But soon discovered I was in way over my head.
This was serious business. We were given uniforms
The old baggy kind, in which we felt like astronauts,
Except I didn't make the Tyees that first year:
A great injustice because, bad as I was, Robin Reid was clearly worse
And only got chosen because he was a Reid.

Of all the things about town life I could have taken as a challenge
I don't understand how I chose hardball. I was certainly just as bad
At any number of more important things including school itself
But nobody asked me to do well at baseball.
I harassed my mother into buying me a mitt
Which of course she cheaped out on, but I got a threadbare ball
And chucked it into the pocket about 10,000 times
Never improving it noticeably. I chucked rocks on the walk home
For hours, once narrowly missing Dorothy Gough, who was not amused.
I got a little book by Bob Feller and studied how to pitch
And made the team the second year, when I was overage
But it was a small town and the other coaches made allowances

/ 23

I'm sure they wouldn't have if I was any good.
Of course they stuck me in right field at first.
Terrified when someone finally hit a short, high fly,
I tried to triangulate my way underneath it
But miscalculated by about ten feet, grabbing crazily at empty air
As it plopped into the grass yards behind me.
"Jeez, that must have been embarrassing,"
Said Gordie Gough, never slow to rub it in

I wasn't athletic. Or if I was my skills were in things like rowing,
Log birling, cliff climbing and bushwhacking.
I could go through undergrowth or up a tree like a marten:
Running on flat ground was just something I'd never done.
But baseball is a sport where a kid can survive by his wits
And by my third season they moved me to left field
And even put me at second base occasionally.
I loved it. I had never experienced improvement so tangibly,
Never knew the thrill of achieving something so entirely on my own.
In time I played every position but catcher, and did my turn at pitching.
Never did master hitting worth a damn
But became such a master of triangulating myself under flies
I'd hear coaches telling their hitters, "Keep it away from left,"
And the coach once singled my dad out in the Legion
To say he'd only every seen one other kid
Who was as good at running down flies.

I can still feel a little swell of pride as I re-enact
Some of those liners I nabbed at the edge of the foul track
And the time I threw a batter out from deep right field.
It did for me everything team sports are supposed to do
And gave me the ability to relate to the greatest athletic achievements

Even though my career was over at 14
When it became too difficult to find enough boys to play
And I went on to the rest of life full of the inner conviction
I could do just about anything if I went about it
The same way I went about my career in baseball.

THAT FIZZY FEELING

When I was a little boy I used to get this fizzing feeling
Whenever someone praised something I'd done
And also when someone stroked or patted me
But only if I sincerely felt I deserved it
I imagined the blood in my arms and back and scalp
Was fizzing with tiny bubbles like shaken pop
It wasn't exactly pleasant but something
Made me think this was what life was all about
This was the frisson, the essence, the t'zin of living
Although I didn't know any of those words then
And am not sure t'zin means what I need it to mean
I only know it because I saw it on the gatepost
Of Hubert Evans, a wonderful man who I credit
For having about as much of this righteous fizz
As any person I ever met
Once when I was still in Green's Bay
And working mindlessly away at my chores
Singing made-up cowboy songs
Thinking I was alone
A funny old tourist guy caught me in the act
I still remember his name: Peter Trappitt
—Peter and Gladys—
They weren't typical tourists
With a fancy Chris Craft from Seattle
They actually lived nearby in Pender Harbour
And had a little converted lifeboat
Upon which they rigged an ungainly canvas top
Like a floating version of a covered wagon
That even then I knew was hokey and cheap

/ 26

We didn't know quite what to make of the Trappitts
They seemed to have nothing better to do
Than poke around the coast's busy logging camps
In their funny bargain-basement boat
Catching little boys singing mindlessly away
And saying *My, that's a wonderful song*
And giving me such a large dose of fizziness
It must have been visible to their old, keen eyes
Maybe I rubbed my scalp or something
Because when it came that strong it was almost like itching
Anyway somehow I ended up trying to explain
All about the tiny bubbles surging upward under my skin
And how it almost hurt but was nevertheless good
And I remember how amazed they both were
And I think even said this was the most extraordinary
Thing they had encountered on all their travels
Which puzzled me, that such a barely real thing could be so big
Although as the years have passed
I have come to see their point
And long to get that fizzy feeling once again
Though it has come to me less and less
And it has been years now since I last got it
I don't know what it would take at this point
Maybe if I won the Nobel Prize
And this poem was cited as the reason

MY TO-DO LIST

By mistake opening my to-do list
I realize I haven't thought of it in weeks
It sits there in my Google Drive
Like forgotten perishables in the fridge
Silent and uncomplaining
With its urgent duties all so overdue
As to be no longer urgent
All lost causes now
Gone to join how many more
Like my in-basket contents
That mound up accusingly
Until in a panic to make my desk presentable
I heave them into the closet where
They moulder into scandal
Then finally vaporize in irrelevance
Leaving my life apparently unharmed
Though I wake up at night in deep despair
At the thought of some celestial tally-sheet being kept
The only escape from which seems to be
To get up full of desperation
And set off in some wholly new direction
With a fresh new harvest of commitments.

TECHNIQUE

Most people don't believe technique makes all that much difference.
If you get the gist of it that's all that really matters
And anybody with half a brain can take it from there.
Which works just fine for things like writing poems
But we can still be amazed at the simplest sleight of hand
From kids' card tricks to the feats of the Amazing Kreskin.
What if Kreskie said, "Close is good enough,"
And sawed right through the Lovely Sheba,
Guts and blood all over the stage? That would not be good.

I am fairly good at pouring.
I seldom use a funnel.
I have studied the disposition of liquids and unguents.
Before tilting the pitcher I fire up my intuits
And picture how that 90 lb gear lube is going to pour
In this minus 2 degree weather. Sluggish. *Very* sluggish.
It will ball up in the spout, forming a bulb of goo
Which will then tumble out pulling a long thin string.
I have to be ready for that. I'll have to dial back
Just before the blob breaks free so it is reduced
Just enough to slip through the too-tiny filler hole.
Then the rest will be easy if I just hold steady and pour slow.
Sometimes I let it pile up a little just to watch the crazy way
The thick liquid folds over itself stitching rapid zigzags,
Balancing on the knife-edge of total backlash,
Tempting fate for my own idle amusement

If there were an Olympic event for pouring
I bet I would get at least to the quarter finals.

Unfortunately that is one of my few skills.
I never learned how to make that ear-shredding whistle
Using two hands. I know only basic Word commands.
I always thought I was a good driver
Until I hitched a ride with that engineering student
Who went into controlled skids on every corner
And cut my time to Sechelt right in half,
Left my ears throbbing from the screeching of tires
But never once crossed the line of real danger.
Of course you need an MG to do that.
I remember Sam Hately, a gorilla of a man
Whose feats were of the brute strength kind
Speaking admiringly of a young surgeon he met
Who used to knot threads inside a matchbox
Just for practice, a mini Houdini.
I can only make blobby welds on the flat
But Hilary Peach can stitch perfect seams even over her head
That betray not the slightest flaw when x-rayed.
So much of this world depends on technique,
On infinite, patient care finally ending in magic,
I wonder what we couldn't accomplish
If we only took that same painstaking approach
To some of the things that really matter.

ROMANCING THE GNOME

When I was in college
I found myself using a lot of 'therefores' and 'it will be seens'
And turning into a kind of pencil-neck
Who only ever thought in abstractions
I found myself increasingly nostalgic
For my old logging camp self
Who only ever thought in terms of logs
And truck loads per day
I was drawn to writers like Ernest Hemingway
And William Saroyan
Who possessed a type of wisdom
My professors dismissed as "gnomic"
But gnomic or not
I set out to get it
Worried I would never be able to slough off
This elevated way of talking
My university days had marked me with.
It took a long time but I think I finally did it.
Now I am back where I was
With the worm's eye view looking up
At all the fancy talkers
Who don't know where they're going
Me trying to avoid getting stepped on

STREET DANCE

Has anybody seen my joie de vivre?

I must have left the damn stuff around here somewhere
I'm trying to think when I last had it
I think it was sometime in the seventies
I remember one night coming down Jervis Inlet in moonlight
I am quite sure we both had it there
Because we decided to get married shortly after

Not absolutely sure I've seen it since
I did go back up Jervis to see if I could find it
And while pleasant enough (especially in retrospect)
I'm pretty sure the joie meter never got above medium
It has occurred to me to do some buying of leisure items
And I've dropped a lot of cash in Canadian Tire and Costco
And even Sun Tours to search around the world
But damned if I can find it anywhere
I just read this one-eyed woman reporter
Who got bombed in Syria had plenty of it
And I wonder if that is what you'd have to do,
Go on a do-good suicide mission to find it
Or if she had the joie first and it took her there

I did always intend to track down Zorba the Greek
But I guess with the bankruptcy of Greece that's too late
It could be one of those things like your shadow
That if you look too hard you'll never find it
Or is it that you just get so used to it you cease to see it

/ 32

I am a bit of a laggard in this search I admit
Compared to some elderly friends who wear out
The Himalayas with hiking and biking and ashramming
But I am not sure they are getting any more than me
To judge by the vivre of their overlong digital slideshows
The closest I came lately was when I was at Canada Day
With my three-year-old granddaughter when the street band struck up
And she pranced past her Mom and Dad and Gran
To select me to dance her in the street
I had never actually danced in the street before
But felt it was an honour I could not decline
I may have caught a glimpse of it then
As her innocent glee
Spilled a little on me

JANUARY 1, 2016

Looking over my list of 2015 New Years Rezzes
I am appalled by the relatively easy vows
That remain pristinely untouched
In fact several new ones I think quite original and smart
I discover I have been listing for the past three years
It seems 2015 never got out of the starting blocks
And here it is over already
I curse the mechanical memory of MS Word
For getting me in a funk before this year is even started
Until I click along to my My Pictures file
Thinking there won't be much to see
Since I have pretty much worn out
The initial thrall of digitizing every moment
And apparently nothing happened last year anyway
But wait—here in January is grandson Cal
Warming in the Mexican sun at six weeks of age
It was sure no forgettable year for him
Or for his sleep-deprived but ecstatic parents
With their overworked iPhone cameras
Clicking on April, there is the hand-scrawled birthday card
Given to me by my two little granddaughters
For my birthday, which come to think of it
Marked the expiration of my three score and ten
Which I tried to defy with this selfie atop Mt. Daniel
The May folder contains my dear old papa
On his 101st, skeletal and pale but still twinkling
And how could I forget, among the many broken
Promises of the year, we finally made good on our
Decade-old plan to place a float in the May Day parade!

/ 34

Here are the grand-girls cavorting in the blow-up pool
Amid a blizzard of bubbles, and also climbing trees,
Roasting wieners, hunting treasure—
I guess we didn't entirely neglect them after all
Rounding into October, here is a difficult shot
Of my great and beloved papa
Minutes before he made his exit from
What he insisted on calling, despite its slow moments,
The Greatest Show on Earth

NATURE FACTS

I would like to dispel a commonly made charge
Namely that I am a know-nothing about nature

It's true I don't know the Latin name of anything
Except *Gaultheria shallon*, the noxious salal bush
And the wonderful *Oncorhynchuses*, *keta* and *nerka*
Otherwise dog and sockeye salmon but the worth
Of knowing names is now greatly devalued by
Google, especially if you have a smart phone

No, the kind of nature I have come to know is
Don't park your car under a wild cherry tree in May
Or you will spend a whole morning removing the gum
(Actually it washes off not bad if you get it before it bakes on)
Also a lot of people think deer are mute. They're not.
When driven to it they can trumpet like an elephant.
They are also quite violent, though that has been on YouTube.
What else? How many know that here on the raincoast
We have a variety of boa constrictor
A pocket version shy to an extreme, the gorgeous green rubber boa
You can wear it like a necklace
And feel it harden as you stroke its velvety scales
Most experts live and die and never see one
Outside a herpetarium, though it has been my luck
to have seen and caught two
And did you know crabs can swim
You betcha the big boys can, the cancer crabs we call "eating crab"
Sometimes you'll hear a swishing beside the dock
And here will be this foaming commotion and it's a big heavy crab

Thrashing its way to the surface, god knows why
Maybe to avoid a fight
They fight like crazy, you know
You'll see them going at it like crazed knights in armour
Biting each others' legs and biters off, oh they're vicious
And now for the weirdest wild fact of all: the roaring bullhead.
There's this little fish, some relative of the bullhead clan
That can make the weirdest and loudest racket
An electrical humming that sounds like a bad transformer
About to blow, so if there's one in a bay every captain in that bay
Will be searching his bilge in a panic fearing conflagration.
We used to have them in Bargain Harbour and I thought
There must be a short in the underwater cable to Edgecombe Island
Until old Jim Warnock, that repository of raincoast lore,
Laughed and said, "That's just a roarin' bullhead, that's all that is!"

Once I took some nature-minded tourists from Australia
For a walk in the little wilderness park next door
Quite worried that they would ask obvious questions
And my ignorance about my own home turf would be exposed
But it worked out quite the other way—
I was able to provide common names for all the trees and bushes
Point out the other-worldly-looking groundcones
That I somehow knew had a parasitic relationship with salal
And also that First Nations used to snack on them
These folks were highly impressed by my local knowledge
And through their eyes I suddenly looked a whole bunch smarter
Also to myself, so comforting to see the occasional sign
One's daily walk about this planet may not have been
Quite so distracted and uninstructive as previously thought

SYMPATHY

I'm a poor mourner.
I never make the hard phone call
Or even send the sympathy card,
Thinking that's their business, not mine,
Even though I know how good it was
To receive cards when Mum died.
We displayed them like Christmas cards
Counted the ones from strangers double
And the ones not sent by friends double negative.
So I know better but I still dodge my duty.

Tell me what it is makes me do this?
I'm not a lazy guy really, here I am
Writing on and on about it later.
I'm not an uncaring guy, I don't think,
Though I can't produce any proof for that.
So what is it makes me turn away
From the pain of real suffering?
You'd think as a guy who complains
About the barrenness of modern life,
I'd value a chance to feel some real feeling.
I know that's what it is but I think that's it—
Real feeling. I crave it, but when I find it
I am so unprepared I turn away.

Also there is the fact I have
Stripped my life clean of ceremony
All is ad hoc and unscripted with me
Nothing rehearsed or rehashed

If I can help it and that leaves me
Feeling the feelings but without
Ready moves or words to show them.
I look with disdain on all the speakers
Of trite words of comfort,
Leaving these most crucial communications
To the writers of Hallmark cards.
Once I attended an Indian Shaker funeral
Where the mourners clanged a loud bell
To induce the Shakers to start shaking
But despite the fact there were expectant dignitaries there
Or perhaps because of that, the Shakers couldn't shake
And put their bell away rather than fake it
But not before passing around a can
To collect money to pass out to all the witnesses
(They came back after we left and had a real good shake)
And I thought that was maybe a better way,
So opposite our orgies of false feeling.

But really, whether it's ritual keening
Or sticking flowers on a crowd-control fence
It is all just ritual, prefab gestures
To acknowledge what words can't say
And what is wrong with that?

2.

MUNGA

FRANKLIN WETMORE WHITE
(1914-2015)

THE OLD MAN PLANS HIS MEMOIR

I want to lay it all out here, all the things I've done, all the
houses I've built, all the rusty mufflers I miraculously saved for
another month, all the naily boards I recycled, all the logs I put
in the water, all the gallons of gas I sold, all the miles of ditch I
dug and laid with pipe and filled in again, all the loads of gravel
I hauled—I'd like to use this book to mound it all up in one huge
mountain beside a huge lake of all the milk I lifted up into my
truck, hauled, lifted down again at the Greeks—I'd like to lay
that all out here and say, okay that's my contribution, that's what
I did with my life, and take pride in just being the guy who did
all that. But I can't get away from the fact I didn't do it for its
own sake, I did it to get rich and I didn't get rich, and that
undercuts it. It leaves me feeling like it was all for naught, like I
spent my whole life barking up the wrong tree or going down the
wrong path. I know the free enterprisers would say that's fine,
that's the beauty of the free enterprise system—for every
millionaire who actually cashes in there's a million guys like me
working their guts out in the hope of something they don't get,
can't get, or else the system wouldn't work. If everybody got the
brass ring, then it wouldn't be worth having and all this
productive effort would cease. They think that's just fine, having
millions of old guys like me sitting here thinking, "Damn, I
missed out." But I have to wonder at a system that can only
survive by causing most of its participants to end in failure.
Maybe it works, but it's not the perfect system. But as an
evolutionist, I have to admit the success of the survivor is built
on the failure of the majority who became extinct. And those
who became extinct didn't really become extinct, they passed
their genetic material on to the species that made the fine

/ 43

adjustments that allowed them to survive. Ninety per cent of our genes are still the old tree rat that disappeared without leaving any other trace. And ninety-nine point nine of my grand children's genetic material is only there because me and Kay and the other grandparents struggled along and brought it to them. That is finally what it's all about and that has to be good enough. This is what I think as I sit here in my lift chair watching the sun set over Texada.

MUNGA'S METHODS

i

Don't sweat the small stuff.
This is my main motto and sometimes I think I have pursued it to my harm
But when I hear what people say are my good qualities, most of them
Come back to my *modus operandi* of not being a by-the-book guy,
Of being a free thinker and a random sort of person.

ii

Sneak away.
I could never schedule my life so I had regular leisure hours or holidays
So I developed this way of stealing breaks in between my day's jobs.
If I had to go to town to get parts, I'd slip out to visit my old Aunt Bess
    in Maple Ridge
Or I'd take the long way home and stop and watch a beaver build its dam.
This would snap me out of whatever rut I was in,
Worrying about where to find the next gas payment.
I did this as a habit and it made me late for a lot of suppers.
My wife learned to accommodate me and make
The kind of slapdash dinners I deserved.
People start to make room for you.
It becomes part of your identity,
Which makes life easier.

iii

Work in from the edges:
If you can't chop a big knotty block of firewood in half,

/ 45

Start working in from the edges splitting off small chunks (go with the grain)
Eventually you will get the block down to where you can crack it.
Do I need to mention this approach works for most of life's big knotty
   problems?

iv

Time is the number one resource and also the most misused resource.
Most of my life I acted like time was endless but here I am,
I have at the most a couple years left and maybe only a couple days.
Every minute counts, but I try not to think about that because it just
   paralyzes you.
It's best not to watch the clock.
If you stare at an egg waiting for it to boil it can take an hour.
But if you turn away and clean off the countertop
Or put out the garbage, the egg will boil instantly.
I wish I had more insights as true as that one.
The more time drags, the faster you use up the time you have.
When I look back at that stupid, boring Water Board job,
I can't believe I spent 15 years at it because I barely have one memory
   from it.
But when I look back at the time I ran the gas station,
It seems like it must have gone on for 20 years even though it only went o:
For 4 years. But it was challenging and eventful and stressful, so it
   stretched time.
Same with Green Bay. Running my own logging camp.
It only lasted 5 years but it seemed to take up the whole middle part of m
   life.
Every day took everything I had in me.
Every year I spent there was worth ten normal years
Which is not to say they were good years.

/ 46

OLDTIMER

The Oldtimer, as my brother and I called him,
Spent a lot of time enraged at our mum
Then when she died he felt his life was not worth living.
The loss was beyond imagining.

It was like a whole piece of himself was gone,
The largest piece, and what was left was not worth anything.
And here he had been thinking
She didn't mean anything to him anymore, she was a throwaway.

What happens to couples that they get like this?
They grow together like two trees with intertwined roots,
Feeding each other the essence of life
Yet in their minds they think they're separate.

They grow numb to their conjoined state
View each other distantly, thinking they could do better
Alone.
Then they do separate through death or divorce,

Suddenly they are left gasping for life.
It is such a surprise to them
That their partner meant that much.
They wonder how they ever could have been so wrong.

FAULTY ASSUMPTIONS

I grew up thinking my dad was like all men
Not that I knew many other men but I read books
And I thought he probably screwed around on my mum
He was always flirting with carwives at the gas pumps
And you can see they thought that Frank is a card
So it wasn't hard for me to imagine them
Ripping off a quick one up some logging road
Like old Wimpy Wallace and Mrs. Markle that time
Our Junior Forest Warden troupe surprised them
But then later when Pop was older and my mum dead
And we were having a drunken tell-all talk
I asked him outright and he said no,
He had never once cheated on Mum in 40 years
And in fact the only one time he ever had illicit sex
Was with old May Whatzername, you know, Ernie Dingbat's wife
We were in the back room of the shop one time
Rooting around looking for muffler parts
I just reached out and put my hand on her ass
Don't know what came over me, it was just sticking out there
So she says okay, and we get in the car
And go down in Tyner's old driveway there
It was alright but neither of us wanted to do it again
But that was the only time since before I met Kay
And I could tell he was telling the truth.
He told the truth too much, that was one reason
He never got anywhere, at least anywhere he wanted.
So this caused quite a revision of the assumptions
I had lived by for my first forty years or so
Now I had to figure out a whole new theory of the universe
Something I would just as soon not have had to do.

MUNGA'S FINAL THOUGHTS ON THE MATTER

Here's what was stupid. The last way to make money is by working for it. It actually costs you money because all the time you have your head down in that ditch you're missing out on all the money going by on the street. I can drive down the road here in Pender Harbour in any direction and count off properties that guys begged me to buy off them for fifteen hundred, a thousand bucks that are now worth a million. I wouldn't have even had to pay the thousand, all I would have had to do was go to the credit union and put down a hundred and re-route my beer money for a few years, just one of these waterfront lots, and I would have made more money than I did working in all the years since. I could have done it even if I'd started only ten years ago. Even if I'd kept the life insurance policy I cashed in to live off when I was 50, I would now have half a million to pass onto my great grandchildren. If I had taken that $1,500 I put into that old Case backhoe in 1959 and instead put it into blue chip stocks, I would be a multimillionaire right now. I don't like to think about it, it makes me feel like everything I did instead of doing that, all that struggle and strife, was a complete waste of time. So a man ends up trying to rationalize it. I tell myself, if I had actually made money I wouldn't have known how to handle it, I would have become an even worse drunk than I was and probably forced my wife to leave me, and the money would have given her a good incentive to do so, she would have taken the kids with her and all the satisfaction I have now from having this wonderful bunch around me I wouldn't have. That may or may not be true. I don't see why it has to be that way. Most of the guys I know who did make money I wouldn't trade places with, but there must be some guys somewhere who handled it alright.

But there's another way to look at it too. That is, what's a guy going to do with his life? You've got to do something. Life is goddamned long and you have to fill all those days up with something. It's a bigger problem than you might think. Almost every person I know who got themselves in a position where they didn't have to struggle to survive ended up going silly. Every damn one. The picture is so clear you can't just dismiss it. And what it comes down to is you have to have something to make you get up in the morning, something you believe you absolutely have to do, not as a matter of choice but of necessity, or else your life just backs up and turns to pus. The human animal spent millions of years developing in a dog-eat-dog evolutionary battle and came out on top of that bloody heap as the meanest, deadliest competitor of them all. Most of our DNA comes from that, the modifications that have happened during the forty thousand years of civilization are insignificant, and you have to keep in mind, that's what's inside us, that's what drives us. I know, because for the last twenty years that is what I have had—the life of leisure, and I wouldn't trade one of these golden years for the worst year I spent busting my ass making a living as a younger man, when I at least thought I was doing something. So there. That ought to about settle it. But still you keep wondering and regretting everything, and cursing your luck. And that's part of life too, I guess. Oh, there's more to it, people who have had nothing to do for generations and generations adapt to it like those old English snobs who refused to work and thought it was demeaning even to engage in "trade." They had their parlour games and society and fox hunting and art—and war mongering, don't forget the ultimate sport. But does anybody really look at the English upper class today with any kind of

/ 50

envy? They're more in the museum of freaks. Imagine being sent off to boarding school as soon as you could bloody well walk, to be brought up by servants who weren't English gentlemen themselves but were thought to know the recipe for making gentlemen and could give it to you like a uniform. And who in a lot of cases were themselves totally screwed up as human beings, except they had this job they had to do, turning scared little abandoned children into proper upper class snobs, and that kept it at least a little bit honest. And yet that is still the model we admire: there is still nothing that's really replaced the British blue-blood as the ideal of the perfect western person. This just shows how lost we really are. We all aspire to something that we know, when we stop to think about it, is a bad joke. But that's not the only model for the idle classes. There's lots of other versions of genteel living: there's your old southern plantation people and your New England Harvard types, if they're really different, I don't know, but they have a lot of the same idea of cultivating leisure and going after the finer things in life and you have to give it some credit. I don't think I could have survived the last 20 years if I hadn't run into a woman who had a lot of skill for handling idleness and took me on all these trips and had all these dinners with amusing people and all that. On the face of it it looks like it should have been the crowning reward of my life when I sort of got the dream—a beautiful, accomplished woman who showed me all the great sights and introduced me to many of the great people of my time, or at least enough representative samples you can kind of guess at the rest. And it's been great, don't get me wrong. I had a second chance, I got to make up all the things I'd missed in my own life. But would I trade one of these years of drifting around asking myself if I'm having fun yet for one of those early years when I was getting up at five a.m. to

/ 51

go up and pit myself against some make-or-break problem in some forgotten logging slash, feeling absolutely convinced I had to do it to keep my world afloat? In my heart of hearts I have to say I wouldn't trade one of those days when I was a man among men battling it out for a hundred of these later days of ease. There you have the mystery of existence.

DENOUEMENT

Looking after my old man during his decline
Through his nineties and finally past 100
I expected to be an unpleasant duty
And it definitely had its messy parts
But overall it was very enjoyable,
Definitely brought us closer than ever
Even though he was a shadow of the man he'd been.

It was very educational, not just
In instructing me in the care industry
Trouble getting up? Buy a lift chair.
Legs get tired standing at the stove?
There's a thing like a walking-stick seat
You can move around the kitchen.
Afraid of falling in the tub?
There's a $1000 gizmo to ease you up and down.
Can't stand at all any more?
Time to move to a power wheelchair.
Trouble loading peas onto the fork now?
They have a big spork that comes with
A special plate with a fence around it.
But really it's better to put everything in wraps or rolls.
Can't even manage that anymore?
Purée everything for easy spoon-feeding.

Like the man said it's a long way down.
But clever technology is waiting at every step
And it's all half price or less on Craigslist.
The thing I really learned, though,

Was how the final stages of life's ending
Form an exact parallel with its beginning:
After nine decades of slow change
Things start moving quickly again.
Every week a changed ability of the body or mind
Creates a whole new situation
Needing altered gear and care strategies.
And the fact your care-receiver
Is changing every day for the worse
Is not as depressing as you might think.
There is something satisfying
About all these long-lost chickens
Coming home to roost.

ESCAPISM

I would like to register a complaint about the way
This brain I've been given so often shies away
From the real thing it should be thinking about
Like right now the thing you'd think I'd be writing about
Would be the biggest thing that happened lately
Namely the death of my dear old dad only last month
But I don't think I've written one line about that
Instead writing about shopping habits
The change of the federal government
The latest charming tricks of the grandchildren
This is a habit not only of my mind but one
I have been frustrated by so many times
For instance by that poet who worked in a pulp mill
But wrote only about his weekend nature walks
Or the cab driver who wrote about crackpot politics
Instead of the nightmare world of the city night shift
I think I can muster some sympathy for him now
Thinking of that gaping death mask
How it stops thought cold, too much to process
Making my mind slide away to more manageable thoughts

NOT SHOOTING POP

My dear old pop, when he was not so old or so dear either,
And spied some older guy struggling along
In a wheelchair mumbling to himself and smelling of pee
Often said stuff like I hope you'll shoot me
Before I ever get like that

But he did get like that and worse and I didn't shoot him
He lasted until he was 101, until
He was down to, in his own words,
Nothing but eyeballs and asshole
Floating on rubber bubbles in a special bed
Being eaten away by rampaging bedsores
Voice reduced to a breathy husk
None of us in the family could decipher
Able only to communicate with his Filipina care aide
Using a system of eyeblinks and ESP
The translation lost in her mangled English
And even then I was not tempted to shoot him
Or leave his bottle of Oxycontin out
For a swift, dreamy exit from all that misery
Not that he would have availed himself
His minutes becoming more precious
As he had fewer of them.

3.

TWO WAYS TO BE BRILLIANT

WHARVES

Here on the coast you can judge a family
by the condition of their wharf
Some have sloping slimy half-sunken things
held together with strings
you would hesitate to tie a canoe to
while others have robust timbered affairs
lag-bolted and chained fit to hold a freighter
Ours is somewhere in between
a bit unorthodox and built of salvage
but sound enough withal
though the near-shore float is now starting to list
and the main one is covered in grass
The ramp too is frilled with lichen

and slippery to walk on: I know every time I do
I think, we're going to have to replace all this eventually

I'm sure my brother does too
though we have not given voice to our concern

Meanwhile I enjoy the fabulous underwater growth
of anemones, chicken of the sea and purple sea slugs
whenever I go swimming, the wharf
getting more interesting as it gets more infirm
unlike its owners

PARENTS

Looking after Martin, 1.7, for one day
Both Mary and I were physical wrecks
To say nothing of being mentally exhausted
It was the best day we could remember
And we were both left to shake our heads
At the thought of his real parents
Doing this all day every day
Which is why you can tell a parent
Just by the way they walk down the street
They are like soldiers
Returned from a 20 years' war
That took everything out of them
But also replaced it with something greater.
They are the only complete humans
Because, face it, this is the great task
We evolved to do
This is what our genetic coding is all about
This is what that trillion-celled brain is wired up for
And it's only when you take on the great challenge
You find out just how much you can really do
How patient you can be, how intuitive
How loving
It is why all veteran parents roll along
With the life-rounded ease of river rocks
Gaze out with a certain satisfied resignation
Beyond all shock or awe
They have been through the wars
They have had shit under their fingernails
They have seen it all

THE SECRET OF THE PYRAMIDS

Is not how did they build them without forklifts
Or even wheels which wouldn't have been much good
In all that soft sand anyway
There is some kind of historical chauvinism
At work here that makes us marvel
That any other age but ours was ever able to
Make anything big, be it the pyramids
Or the Great Wall of China or the Roman Coliseum
(Which could get lost in the sprawling ruins of Angkor Wat)
Some would say the secret was slavery
Or agriculture, which freed workers to
Spend their time doing frivolous things
But if you think you can build even a
Good outhouse by forcing people to work
Against their will, you have probably never tried
No, you won't get anything to amaze the ages
Through sheer nastiness
That only gets you Walmart

If you want to blot out the sky or make
Something so astonishing or stunning
It bids the rash gazer wipe his eye
Then you have to let your workers do it their way
Give them their head and let them go
They will go beyond themselves if you let them
I have seen it on every team I was ever part of
At a certain point they either get cooking
And take the job in hand or the thing is a disaster
Like the crumbling bridges of Montreal

/ 61

Where corruption at the core defeats the will to work
There is no worse feeling than to be working
On a job where the bosses don't care
Call it *esprit de corps* or whatever you want
Service, duty, purpose—it is that use
That brings all our systems right
Makes all unworthy preoccupations vanish
Unleashes that thirst for fulfillment
In doing what we can, giving all
A job must reach a point where it jells
And all the workers lay to with a will
Knowing just what they have to do
And really trying to do it the best way they can
It is not so hard to achieve: you don't have to be
Churchill or Ataturk or Alexander the Great
Workers will put out for an absolute bastard
If only he gives them the tools and shows them respect
They will buckle down and do the rest
Raising 20-ton blocks to the skies with only sweat and smarts
Just to prove something
To themselves

FREE TICKETS TO RON SEXSMITH

We took a couple free tickets to see a concert
By a third-order Canadian music star
We would never have paid to see named Ron Sexsmith
And now I can't stop thinking about him.
I'm not sure exactly what it was

That made his performance so memorable
He couldn't pen an earworm at gunpoint
He is just this middle-aged musician
From a small city outside Toronto
Who never made it big
For all that he has been praised by
Some of the biggest names like Elton John
And boy, does he ever know it
He introduces songs by saying
"Here's another one that really bombed"
"This is from an album that didn't sell"
And yet there he stands, singing his heart out
Sweating so hard he has to use a bath towel
Barely stopping for a breath between songs
Which are not just beautiful and complex
But so unlike anything any other singer sings
You can tell before he's sung three words it's him
You'd think if he cared so much about making it
He would have tried to sound more like Neil Diamond
But no, he stayed with this lovely but weird sound
Ever since his very first album when he was
Crisscrossing this wide empty country
Singing his ass off like a blinded canary or whatever

There is something about the very doing of that
I find almost more moving than his impressive art itself
An acceptance of his role as a minor but true note
Sifting its way through all the cacophony of our distracted age

LOVE

A girlfriend once asked me what was the best sex I ever had
To which of course the only safe answer is "this one"
But instead I went into a long dissertation
About all the different contenders for the title
Which is probably why she is an ex-girlfriend
But really you have to admit it's hard
To rate something so over-the-top as orgasm
It's like rating the times you've been knocked unconscious
Heaven blazing into the head is pretty much
Heaven blazing into the head
There is a finality to it that defies ranking
Like taking a shot of grain alcohol
White light contains all colours
All stories.
That's one way of looking at it.
The other way is looking at the setting and circumstances
Some were with dangerous dames in strange hotels
Some were with old lovers familiar as worn shoes
Some were in beautiful outdoor settings
Some were snapped off standing up
Some were stretched out for deliberate hours
You can spend days reflecting over which miracles
Arrived in the best wrapping

RACCOON PASS

Thank you, Peter and Lisa, for taking me to this place
Which will now be with me for all my days
Swimming back into mind with images
Of the lake's incredible turquoises blending to rust
The ribs of light moving over it like an ethereal conveyor belt

In my much-begrimed life it has been long, too long
Since I have been able to simply stop and wonder
At merely material things like ribbons of spray
Dripping from peaks all around us
One I could have ignored maybe—but a dozen
Whose combined roar keeps up day and night—
That breaks through even my crusted indifference

And clever too, to make me stay here for a whole week
To let the sheer force of visual and physical impacts
Hammer their way into my dried-up soul
Break it open and find some juice in there still

We kept exploring every day, making those distant peaks
Come close so that by the time we left we could look
At inviolable crags and say we were there on Wednesday
Making this wild and unknown masterpiece our own
All its yawning glaciers, all its foaming rivers
All its surprisingly placid pools and beds
Of brilliant wildflowers I feel no need to name

And above all that inimitable feeling of being out of one's skin
Of being reduced to sleeping, eating, shitting, drinking

And putting one foot in front of another steadily but safely
Through all the stages of exhaustion and out the other side
To a place above all the clogging underbrush of common life
Where a brilliant clarity rains down on the world.

ODE TO A STUMP

Grand old relic of days gone by
Of my father's time and my father's work
Rising bravely from the mossy carpet
Tall as a monument to someone great
Bark thick as grizzly fur, now almost as soft
The telltale notches climbing up like stairs
Where the old handfallers stood on springboards
Working through a morning of chopping and sawing
Feeling they were doing something great
All worries cast in shadow for the moment
Striving toward that epic screech and howl
Of greatness crashing down
Setting the whole harvesting process in motion
So men like my dad could fire up their machines
And move that wood on out to the mills
I have lived surrounded by stumps
The great old first-growth cedars and firs
The more recent smaller ones
Stepped and tufted by powersaws
And for most of my time felt affection
Marking the passage of my kind
Through the cold wilderness of green
Only in recent years come to have qualms
About the sheer number and impersonality
Of vast fields of ever-smaller stubs
As corporate efficiency changed everything
And the once-trackless ocean of bush
Shrunk back to crevices and corners
Nor can I ignore the tide of disapproval

Washing in from the cities, leveraged by media
That redefines these symbols of our way of life
As images of wanton destruction and rapine
A view I can't wholly dispute or reject
While still convinced it misses something

NO ORDINARY BILL

Everybody still talks about Blind Bill Hallgren, if they knew him.
Bill had a congenital condition that gave him a hunched back,
And macular degeneration which left him about 90% blind.
He kept getting blinder as time wore on but he kept adjusting
So half the time he seemed to be denying any handicap
And half the time exaggerating his need for every break and benefit
He was one of those loveable scoundrels who soon knew more people
Than I'd met in thirty years of living on Saturna Island.

I recently started thinking of him in relation to Donald Trump.
Bill had a way of playing poker that reminds me of Trump.
He would trash talk and mug and drop his cards and break every rule
And keep losing track of whose bet it was then make crazy raises
And most nights he would go home with the biggest winnings.
The rest of us never caught on: chaos was his comfort zone.

He was an expert mind-fucker. I learned not to get stoned with him
Because he couldn't resist trying to do nasty head trips.
Even straight he loved to get into it with people
Figure out their key beliefs and start picking at them
His tiny wife Janie, who was 100 per cent blind
And had been raised as a kind of delicate flower
But whom he taught to hitchhike and fend for herself
Still had a weakness for attending church
So Bill went along and tried to convert the local Pentecostals
To his own raw-meat atheism, engaging them in epic arguments
As they gave him work and tried everything to prove him wrong

The first I ever heard of Bill he was over in Winter Cove somewhere

/ 70

People were talking about him, young dopers and pub denizens
Giving me the impression somebody loud and bad had moved onto
   the island
Already he was generating intriguing stories
People said he was blind although he was building his own house
Without a building permit and when the building inspector objected
He nailed a plywood prow on his shack and claimed it was a boat
Which effectively confused the authorities who eventually gave up
And let him continue building until he had quite a decent home

Once he talked his way onto a deep-sea freighter as a seaman
And did okay until it came his turn to take the wheel
Of course he couldn't see to keep his course but tried to guess
By listening to the clicks the gyro made when the ship wandered
Carefully steering back until it clicked the other way
So that by morning they were 100 miles off course
And the captain went ballistic but Bill's audacious charm won out
And kept him safely peeling spuds the rest of the way to Shanghai.

Another time he decided to set up in business as a danger tree faller.
His chainsaw was old and cranky so he often borrowed mine
Always expressing dismay at the way I had my chain filed
And setting about to do it the right way, lecturing as he groped,
Which always annoyed me because his semi-blind filing was so bad
My brother used to say, "I see your chain has been filed in Braille."
Fallers run for cover when the tree top begins to shudder and tip
But Bill couldn't see the tree top so stuck his finger in the sawcut
To feel if it was opening or closing, which drove all watchers nuts
But he avoided losing any fingers or putting any trees through any roofs
And we all breathed a sigh of relief when he got bored and moved on

Until we discovered he'd answered an ad for a position as watchman
At a camp way to hell and gone up the coast, taking his fully blind wife.
The place was crawling with grizzly bears who Janie would sometimes
Bump right into as she groped her way to the walk-in freezer
Saying "shoo, shoo," and the grizzlies all duly shooed
Unlike most camp watchmen who stayed drunk on homebrew
And stold & sold everything that wasn't nailed down,
Bill kept busy fixing steps and painting railings
And the camp owners loved him, gave him raises and bigger camps

He took a mail-order course on investing and started playing the market
Drew on his poker smarts and did so well he quit and went investing
    full-time
Even starting consulting for other people which made me glad I was
    broke
But Bill kept doing well, quit smoking, drinking, and playing cards
Bought a suit and got elected to the board of the Boot Cove Credit Union
Hired a real carpenter to spiff up Janie's kitchen and put in a hot tub—
Things seemed to be going well for Bill but he wasn't happy.

He'd always been a bit of a hypochondriac fearing every cramp was cancer
Running off to every doctor because both parents had died of colon cancer
We all teased him about it but he just got more obsessed
Doctors got tired of him pressing phantom complaints and blew him off
Then one day he coughed up blood and it turned out he had real lung
    cancer
Too far along to operate, all they could do was give him morphine
But the pain kept increasing and Bill wanted more than the doctors
    would prescribe

/ 72

So he took his carefully hoarded investments and spent it on street heroin
Spiralling downward until he had to spend his last weeks in hospital,
Beset by withdrawal and panic attacks while the Bible thumpers moved in
And finally got him to agree to a desperate addled conversion
Which they proudly announced along with his obituary notice.

ON THE PASSING OF CAPTAIN UPFUCK

Right off the top I should admit I was not part of the Ed Uchuck fan club
And I had my reasons but yeah, I probably took it a bit far
And no doubt shortchanged him on the things he is being celebrated for
By all the Ed Uchuck fan club now, his supposed saving of the old school-
    house
Which Ian Griffith and I actually had more to do with than him
Though I have to admit he did a lot for the Whaletown music scene
But what I'm here to confess is that despite all my petty grudges
I really do feel something at this passing and here's what it is:

I think of him building his sailboat using the strip planking method
The one him and Dot were living on when we first got to know them
I think of him learning how to be a Boot Cove boat repair guy in mid life
I think of him learning how to be a commercial fisherman after that
And going up and down the coast not catching many fish

But fully mastering that scaly lifestyle, becoming one of the boys
Bird-dogging the coast's lonely old widows and unwary schoolgirls
Leaving a trail of empty beer cans and unpaid bills in his wake
And all his incredible misadventures: the time he was coming through
Surge Narrows late against the tide and encountered an out-of-control
Tug and barge whose towline passed over him, dismasting his boat.

Captain Upfuck they called him and he did his best to live up to it
On land and sea, once transporting his beloved piano
In the back of a pickup without bothering to tie it down
Figuring he could just gentle it along but forgetting
And taking the hairpin at Black Creek much too hard
Out the back goes the piano and down the rockslide

With a final, resounding glissando of broken notes
Then when fishing went all to hell and he adapted
By turning his gillnetter into a makeshift cruise boat
Offering romantic jazz cruises in Nanaimo Harbour
With another just as heavy piano perched atop a sheet of plywood
Over the hatch which collapsed mid-arpeggio
Dumping him and his rhapsodic trilling into the fishy bilge
And buggering up his back for the rest of his life

The Captain Upfuck stories go on and on
And it grieves me to think they will end and fade to naught
But for this poor sample.

TO A UROLOGIST

Wondering why it was taking so long for my annual appointment
I looked my urologist up on the internet and found he was dead
Also that his friends and family called him Zeke
There was a logic to it since he was over eighty
And whenever I told other doctors and nurses I was still seeing him
They always said, My god, is he still seeing patients?
But I liked Dr. Perler. I knew him and he knew me
Not quite in the biblical sense although a case could be made
That he was more familiar with my private parts than any lover
Even including the act of penetration for which he always apologized
As if it were an unexpected and most regrettable event
Unlike other butt-doctors who seemed to take delight
And often uttered whoops like a rugby player going in
There is a peculiar kind of pang knowing someone
With whom I have experienced such intimacy for so long
Is suddenly vanished from the earth.
Whither his knobby finger now?
Who will call me up on cold November mornings to ask
How strong my stream is and if my dick is unkinking
Or tell me with a twinkling eye that
Besides curing Peyronie's Syndrome
800-mg doses of vitamin E can have "other benefits?"
Dr. Perler expended such extravagant care over his small area
It almost made up for the neglect I gave the rest of my health
And leaves me feeling vulnerable and exposed.

TWO WAYS TO BE BRILLIANT

One is you go to Oxford on a Rhodes scholarship
Read the classics in the original
Hone your skills for another decade or two
Still retain your freshness and spontaneity

The other is you drop out, do dope
Open the doors of perception
Don't worry about getting it right
Just do a hell of a lot of it
The digital camera approach
Hope there's one shot in there
That caught a dog driving a car or a spirit moving
That will make deliberate genius look sick
Even if that never happens all is not lost
Your constant stream of dross will mass
To such a degree you will have an inventory of 200 books
And be described as your own universe
The grand smear of your accumulated output
Doing something deliberate after all

AGAMEMNON

One of my first words was Agamemnon. First Greek word anyway.
Back in 1950 yachters venturing into the wilds of the BC coast
Would be surprised to discover this five-year-old ragamuffin
Scampering mink-like out onto the slippery log-boom
Would coax me to come aboard with candies
Try to pry a few words of local colour out of me
Finding my vocabulary limited to a few dozen monosyllables
Except for this 3-cylinder doozy "Agamemnon."
Which came up not because we were discussing Homer
But because we were in a bay off Agamemnon Channel

I could even tell them why it was called that odd, angular thing:
I had heard my mother say it was named after Nelson's ship
A fact I found impressed hell out of tourists
Although I could not have told them who Nelson was
Except he was some old guy with one eye
And the island our camp was on was named after him.
I didn't know if his old tub was a gillnetter or a troller
Though I guessed it was at least a seiner like the *Murpak*
Or maybe a coaster the size of the *Jervis Express*
To get a whole channel named after it like that

I soon found it was productive to turn talk to old Nelson
And the queer name of his boat, which I could even spell
Having figured out it was made up of three small words
Each of which began and ended with the same letter:
AgA. MeM. NoN. For another cookie or two
I could even spell it backwards: *nonmemagA.*

I knew that word inside out
Lived it, made it part of my world like tide and rain
And never quite agreed with George Woodcock
That it was really the name of a mythic Greek king
When he professed as much, much later
When that seaweedy ragamuffin found himself
Beached in the halls of higher learning
Having his native understandings of the world
All undermined.

COITION

Ha! Gotcha. There will be no graphic sex in this poem.
Coition only comes into it as a word, a weird word
That perplexed me as a horny youth trying to figure out
Just what steamy adult mystery was hidden under it.
Seems they used it more in the fifties when
It wasn't so cool to say "sex" in public.
Every time things started to get interesting,
Here would be this faceless cop-out of a word
I read as "koyshin" and knew had something to do with "it"
But imagined as something more complicated
The way the authorities danced so gingerly around it,
This impression was abetted by the dictionary
Explaining it as "sexual congress" which got me thinking
Of portly legislators swarming unappealingly in the nude.
"Intercourse" was another cover-up word that caused me grief.
I could never square its interesting use with its OED definition
Which seemed to indicate nothing more than polite conversation,
A mistake I got straightened out about the hard way
When I suggested my grandmother and I have some
—Vivid confirmation of my language teacher's claim
Sloppy diction can be harmful to your health.

AT THE COFFEE MACHINE

Every day when I make coffee
I think of Jerry and Thora

Because they steered us to
This fancy Italian coffee machine
But also because they would be the ones to do that
Thora with her house of fine tastes
Jerry pooh-poohing it all the time
Ostentatiously eating at greasy spoons
His way of rebelling against his wife
I'm sure he would miss her epic breakfasts
If anything happened to her or
They made good on their numerous break-ups
I love Jerry and Thora as I do few people
Can't understand why they have so much
Trouble loving each other
Oh hell, of course I do
And really to see Jerry nursing Thora
After her hip operation
So devotedly
And her so moved by this unexpected tenderness
You know their love is a deep well
With a tendency to just get messy
On the surface
It does me good to think of them
First thing each morning

TOXINS

Something that gets me about all these dietary nuts
Is that they seem to think we are sick all the time
From absorbing so many "toxins."
Do you absorb toxins? I am not aware of any
Toxins going down my gullet on a daily basis.
And how do you tell if you have just
Sucked down a big blob of toxic material?
And anyway, who gets to pass judgment
On just what is toxic and non-toxic in this world?
These people strike me as the peptic equivalent
Of moral majoritarians, pointing their bony fingers
At every food item they see in their zeal as bad,
The work of various demonic dietary conspiracies.
I guess that makes me a kind of toxic relativist.
Isn't everything a little toxic and a little not toxic?
Oxygen is toxic in high enough concentration.
Or perhaps they are right and we are really
Walking around half sick all the time unawares?
That is an enticing thought: what a superman I would be
If I ever got rid of all these toxins and became
One hundred per cent healthy! It sets me thinking
What are the symptoms of this toxicity that weighs me down
Keeping me from being the terrific performer I never knew?
I had a slight case of the trots last Wednesday:
Maybe that was one of the unheeded warnings
I haven't won the T.S. Eliot Prize yet
Maybe that is another.

NEWS FROM SPACE

Looking at a series of earth photos
Taken from space over the decades
The news is the worst

The earth is visibly browning like
A turkey through smudgy oven glass
It's burning up is what is happening

Smoke everywhere down there
Clearing fires in the Amazon and Yucatan
LA pumping out more smog than ever

China's economic miracle made visible
As a thick blanket of coal smoke
Along with this, an increasing number

Of weather events visible from space
Hurricane Sandy tearing into Jersey
Like a whirling saw blade

An unnamed storm brushing the sands
Of the Sahara out over the Mediterranean
Muddying its pure aquamarine

As the entire planet blurs into a smoky vagueness
Like an old man's clouding memory
Of a life once crisply faceted with possibility

THE SEA OTTER

Furry torpedoes wet teddy bears tearing around like giant amoebas
Out there on the west coast holding place with one stubby leg wrapped
    around a kelp frond
So cute so bad trying to look innocent as they devastate another urchin bed
I don't mind them practising ethnic cleansing on the unloveable urchins
But hey take it easy on the poor old geoducks with their hilarious old
    man dorks
One of mother nature's most withering comments upon the race of men
Cute yeah cute as supersized rats gobbling up every kind of shellfish
    ever invented
Before us righteous destroyers can make a buck hell those little bastards
    are so supercharged
We can't even keep up with our underwater hydraulic strip-mining gear
The sea otter can't help it if it has the metabolism of a 50-pound humming
    bird
And has to eat its own weight twice a day to stay warm in those cold
    west coast waves
But maintains excellent humour as it goes about wreaking havoc on the
    environment
Casually cleaning out populations of balletic swimming scallops
In a single gulping afternoon
Look mummy, they've denuded another ten miles of coastline! Aren't
    they sweet!
Reducing Haida Gwaii's luminescent abalone to the rarity it was
When the first globalists sailed in
Inspiring the Haida and Nootka to exterminate their furry brothers
    within two decades
Fuck the great spirit, we need more beads, more beads, more beads

/ 84

But hey these little devils got great pushback: let your bleeding
    heart guard down
And wham they're back in there like fast-spreading cancer
Putting the world back the way it was

THE BOOK OF EARTH

When I had a garden
My world was changed

And focused on the likeliness of rain
The nutrient level of my soil

What the cabbages were thinking
How much overreaching to allow the rose

Walking down the driveway was
A complicated challenge

Sometimes taking hours
As I checked pulses and listened to

Veiny complaints
Now I walk it in a minute

Having closed the book of earth

APOLOGY TO ALFRED PAGE

I remember when we put out those first issues of *Raincoast Chronicles*
How excited I was at the clever way I had managed to turn the
Ordinary story of my own little home town into literature
And even get the place its first actual recognition in big city newspapers
And how when I approached old Alfie Page, he was furious
And as far as I could tell all the oldtimers were furious

At the time I put it down to some backwoods brand of chauvinism
Resentment at the presumption of a young upstart
Now that I am myself an oldtimer and have to put up with
Lately arrived enthusiasts going at our old stories all over again
And getting them all wrong, I feel like apologizing to Alfie's ghost

It's not the intrusion we mind, it's the lack of respect
Fitting something that was after all too real for words
Into the kind of Procrustean bed that is the best art can do
Leaving a trail of arms and legs and heads in its wake
And a few old men and women shuddering with pain
They are at a loss to explain because
How do you explain something that is so damn obvious
To a generation that has no eyes to see it

BRAINFARTS

My father used to go into a kind of a trance sometimes
When he was standing under the hoist in his garage
Working on somebody's old rustbucket of a car
And he would loudly say to himself
"We'll show the bastards!"
Or sometimes, "Let's go get drunk!"
Or other times, "Kay!"
Which was the name of my poor long-suffering mother
Who was in the office adding up the day's take
Over and over, trying to get it to be more than it was
And knew better than to answer his call
Although sometimes strangers would
Helpfully point out, "Kay, Frank is calling you,"
To which she would smile and say "That's okay."
I was awed and disturbed by these robotic exclamations
Wondering if it was going to get any worse
And whatever unfathomable trauma lay behind them
Would someday erupt into open flame
And consume our semblance of normal life
For I never doubted that such ritualistic utterances
Must be tied to something deep-rooted and profound

Now I find myself issuing the same kind of brainfarts
That I am too embarrassed to put down here
And this time I have a clear interior view
Of where they come from.
In my case at least—and I will bet his also—
It's not the real buried bodies of my own past that cause them
Like the girl I broke up with in first year

/ 91

Who later killed herself
Rather it is thinking of things
Like the time quite recently when
I went to an important meeting with my sweater inside out

I don't know whether to be relieved by this realization
Or appalled

WOODPILE

On a sunny end of March Sunday I stay inside til 4:00
Then hustle outside to clean up that bit of split wood
Which I get stacked faster than expected
So I decide to tackle the overwintered brush pile
Before the summer burning restrictions take hold
And soon I am into it with diesel can and power saw
A plume of opaque grey smoke twice the size of the house
Going up to alarm the volunteer firemen around town
I stagger in at 7:00 covered in sweat and ashes
Sit at the table smelling like an old back-country trapper
My wife smirks knowing I am playing at being
The man I once was and knowing by my own half smile
That I wasn't disappointed with what I found

RETRIEVAL

Now what was that thing I was going to get for Munga?
I thought of it on the way home last night
After I had passed the last place I could get it, Canadian Tire.
It wasn't an essential thing, just a minor everyday item
That nevertheless would make a big difference
To his shut-in life and also my step-mother's life
Because whatever this was I was planning to get two.
Omigawd! It was something I've been forgetting
Regularly for most of the past year, something
My butt is sore from kicking myself over
And yet do you think I can think of it now
So Mary can pick it up on her way past CT today?
It was a household item of use to elderly shut-ins
But not one of those gripper sticks I keep thinking of—
They already have half a dozen good gripper sticks
They never use because they are always lost
Just like their hearing aids, which are always lost
And always getting found by being stepped on and broken.
They must have spent $20,000 on hearing aids by now—each—
But this item was nowhere near that expensive,
Just some personal thing that would ease their lives
And make them think fond thoughts of me twenty times a day
If indeed they could even remember who gave it to them.
But who am I to make slighting references to their forgetfulness?
I know I've got all my readers on the edges of their seats over this
And I know once I do remember you will all be disappointed by
    its banality.
But for me right now it is the greatest mystery in the universe

RELATIVITY

Going by the Sheppards' place on my evening walk
I see a beautiful young woman with long blonde hair
Slip out through the gate and slide into a waiting pickup.

It's too young to be Mrs. Sheppard, so it must be one of their kids
   grown up already
I am not sure how many kids they have or what ages they are
Although they have lived five doors away from us for a good ten years now
And it seems only yesterday they had small children playing in the yard
Now here's one of them going on a date and giving her parents fits
Another whole growing-up has happened with me barely noticing
And yet to that young woman it's no doubt been an eternity
It's been a whole life full of terror and love, so eventful
She will be recounting it to grandchildren years hence
And probably not even mentioning that queer old man
Up at the end of Rondeview Road who wrote things
Unless I yet manage to create some spectacular scandal
Or expire in a particularly gruesome way

I think of my own growing up in this town, how it went on forever
How the other kids in my class still populate my nightmares
Mythic figures that serve as archetypes for everyone I've met since
I have written I don't know how many books detailing that era
Which to me seems like a whole epoch in human evolution
And certainly the watershed period in Pender Harbour history
And yet I know to other older residents of this town
That twenty-odd years must seem like only a blip of time
Something half-glimpsed while walking past
Time opening or shutting like pages of a book

OLD FOLKS AT HOME

Of a Sunday morning the old couple did their duty
The wife surrendering her slack achy body
Trying not to show how much she dreaded this sacrifice
Never suspecting he also had to psyche himself up
Both feeling it was something they had to do
For the household economy
Like vacuuming or paying the bills
And both being right about that
And both equally bored with
The placid passage of their days
Maybe we should go join ISIS, he said
She laughed in spite of herself
Because it was so just like him
The crazy old sixties radical still flashed out

Still made her laugh, which was
More fun than what they had just done
She told him a joke about an old couple
The wife asked for ice cream with strawberries
And the man brought her bacon and eggs
And she said, "You old fool—where's the toast?"
And he laughed at that because
It was so just like her, the innocent
Small town girl still peeping out sometimes
Like snowdrops in a forgotten garden

DEMENTIA

It's not that life is dull
Life is amazing and crazy
It's that our ability to respond dulls

Like right now an amazing thing has happened
Edith has got her mind back
Or partly back
For years she's been in a slow slide
Asking over and over if she has children
How many times she was married
If I am my father's son
Today she phones thanking us
For a red skirt we bought her a year ago
A week ago she wouldn't even have known she was wearing a skirt
Much less how to work the phone
At first she didn't even know Dad died
"Who died?" she kept saying
Now she is fully distraught
And saying she doesn't want to live alone 24/7
She is also harassing me constantly
About having a big funeral for Dad
Which we were hoping to sneak by without doing

This is just like she was ten years ago
And we are all being reminded how much easier
It has been to get along with her since she lost her mind
And instead of rejoicing at this miraculous resurrection
We are all hoping she loses it again soon.

/ 97

5.

THE CONSTANT URGE

MY INFLUENCES

I grew up in a logging camp then a redneck fishing village
Where books were not in a place of social prominence
Although my mom tried to counteract this by accepting
The free books offered by Book of the Month Club
Then ignoring all the angry appeals and accusations
Of broken faith etc. until they calmed down
And sent her another offer, which she would also take
And in this way slowly built a library of Kinnan Rawlings
Du Maurier, Ferber and other 1950s bestsellers
These were my *Mother Goose* and *Robinson Crusoe*
I read *Tortilla Flat* and *Giant* before *Treasure Island*
I have rescued these old jacketless volumes from the attic
And have them proudly displayed beside my college Plato
Knowing this cultural flotsam jacketed my imagination
Like a back alley bird that makes its nest from tinsel and plastic

FASTER THAN A SPEEDING BULLET

When I was in Grade 11 and the world a huge mystery
I wrote a poem that I thought aped "The Waste Land"
Which was still considered very avant-garde then
At least in the little cultural backwater I occupied
I had I guess seen "The Waste Land" in some textbook
But hadn't the foggiest notion what it meant
Still, I got something from it: a message from Africa
Via American slave culture via the St. Louis blues
Via stiff-necked London literary tastemakers
Telling me I could break stuff up, go with the flow
Pull images out of deep subconscious
And not make excuses for it
I had no idea what I was doing, really
And only did it with a sense of preposterous fakery
But looking at that poem fifty years later
I can hear "The Waste Land" clearly drumming through it
I can see the fractured logic working perfectly
Even Eliot's unfortunate pedantry in a footnote
Probably ninety per cent of the innovation that won his Nobel
Absorbed through the pores of an ignorant fishing village kid
Which just shows how fast a new music can move

THREE

Poem of the sturdy milking stool
Work-tested to be just enough
And not too many
At least if sturdily splayed
Two wouldn't do
Four, unnecessary
Trios, troikas
Get the job done
Nothing fancy, no free rides
Strength in simplicity
Poem of third time lucky
Three's a charm
Four for those who want more
Three is enough
For me

SAMPLE

I have the constant urge alright
And I don't think that's anything special
Because I have known so many to have it
Bookless old loggers
Sentimental hairdressers
An intellectually challenged teen
Too many professors to count

But it's the doing that does me in
Sitting before the blank screen
Wondering where all the ideas went
A special kind of pain
Knowing life is out there flowing by
Like the Mississippi River
In flood, houses, pickup trucks
Whole barns swooshing along

I think of all the spectacles missed
All the hilarious moments
Cute baby sayings
Tragic failings of age
The very shape of our times
Glimpsed finally like
A long train going round a curve
Material enough to form a continent
And me able only to retrieve
A few bits now and then
Which nevertheless
Brings great satisfaction
And not a few shouts of encouragement

POETS ON THEMSELVES

Pat says Jake's GG-winning work
Isn't real poetry, just elaborate fakery
Pete says Pat has gone all academic
Hasn't written a good line since the 80s
And all Black Mountain poets
Are robotic formalists.
George says Pete is colourful
But isn't a big-deal poet

Such talk is constant
And always amazes me.
These are the writers who monopolize
The pages of CanLit anthologies
Responsible for some of the most
Beautiful lines in Canadian English
But when it comes to reading each other
Acquit themselves with all the subtlety
Of two curs fighting over a grimy bone.
You could get more reliable opinions
From a smart high school student.

DEATH OF A POET

Ed Dorn is dead.
I know, his mortal self died a long time ago, but he's really dead now.
I heard this yesterday in MacLeod's bookstore, pronounced by
The god of used books, Don MacLeod.

If you want absolute certainty, just listen to Don
Going through a box of used books
"Haig-Brown? Yes, he's the only fishing writer who still sells.
Golf? No, golf is dead. I never thought I'd see the day, but here we are.
Same with resource industries. Let me show you. See that Fraser?
It's been sitting there for months. Used to be if I could get a Fraser
I'd have a waiting list. Same with Drushka. But Griffiths,
I could sell a Griffiths. You should reprint Griffiths,
But Ed Dorn? Defintely not. Nobody asks for Dorn any more
Wouldn't take a Dorn if you gave it to me."

I'm vaguely relieved and it's not just the 'the book
Of mine enemy is remaindered' syndrome: here poor Dorn
Has been consigned to a lower level of hell than that
Remaindered and forgotten, buried, removed
From the antiquarians' list of existence.
No, it's that I had always had this vague sense I had never
Done quite right by Dorn and should catch up on him
Now I am relieved of that burden but I may have a more serious problem
As in "ask not for whom the bell tolls…"

/ 106

FANDOM

Even a writer with as small an output as me
Has trouble dealing with reader comments
I guess I've had ~~a thousand~~ ~~a hundred~~ fifty people or so
Come up and say they liked this or that
Mostly small things I wrote for newspapers
Sometimes more pointed comments by
A few loyal and devoted souls who have
Kept track of my scattered output of longer things
It's always welcome of course but troubling
For a recluse to know how to respond
I often fall back on a world-weary "Thankew"
Wrung dry of all sense of special occasion
Which I am sure must be disappointing
But covers up my unpreparedness for praise
Let me say I'm sorry sorry sorry
I didn't respond in kind, say, "I had trouble
Finishing that one, I had so much more to say"
Or, "That was more fun to write about than live through"
Or, "Do you know the West Coast yourself...?"
It is all part of my determination to curl up in my shell
And make sure life never touches my tender parts

TALKING ABOUT IT

I've always thought a poet who talks too much about his poetry
Is like an old lady who talks too much about her bowels
WHO CARES but that doesn't stop me
From saying the poem's chief virtue is utility.
It is over quickly, both for reader and writer
And it does the job: now I don't have to write a novel
And can get on with browsing the internet
Here is the part some may not agree with: its flexibility
I mean you can use a poem
To capture magic or take out the garbage
To weld the crack of dawn or sing happy birthday
To weigh a piece of air at the top of the sky
Or deliver the world's heaviest clunker
Or like I do a lot, put a marker in place
For somewhere I will probably never get back to

ENOUGH ABOUT THE MOON

The moon does not give a shit.
The moon is a hunk of rock.

Women mean nothing to the moon.
It offers them freezing cold and dust.

The moon does not know or care
Why dogs and poets howl at it from next door.

The moon if anything resents the leash of gravity
That tethers it to its bigger sibling,

Grounding its flight through the stars
In an endless holding pattern

Watching the blue ball slowly go brown
Like watching paint dry.

So give the moon a break.

MRS. FLEMING

I think some times of the books I refused to publish
Not *A Salmon for Simon*, which went on to sell 100,000
I just laugh about that
And the weird book about a talking cat
Not because it was a cat
But because the cat only repeated
What the author had said in her last three books
Of course it sold far better than it should have too
I would turn it down again

No, the ones I wonder about
Are ones I know would not have sold
But I still could have or should have done
Like my old English teacher's memoir
It was dry and tedious
But she had saved my life
At least intellectually speaking

Found me putrefying in that fishing town
Stuck Hemingway and Shakespeare in front of me
Told the whole school that if I was an athlete
I would be an Olympic contender
Got me a creative writing scholarship with Earle Birney
Wrote encouraging letters into my thirties
Keeping me honest by
Expressing slight disappointment

Would it have killed me to do a short run
Of her disappointingly arid life story?

I can only hope she appreciated my position
And rejection was not the reason
She stopped writing me.

ACCIDENTAL CHRONICLER

Scabby Mackay in his self-described Black Hole of Calcutta
Anchored half way up Chatham Channel
An untouchable among the old bush apes
Because of his scabbing 40 years before
But now one of the few rangitangs left to tell tales
Of their wild orgy among the tall trees
Is offset by old Bus Griffiths the gentleman logger
The sacred version of Scabby's profane one
Who spent his latter days carefully recording
The nuances of the logger's craft in the only form
He truly felt comfortable with—the comic book
Then there's Spilsbury—scion of landed gentry
Cast ashore on Savary Island without a pot to piss in
And no school to go to beyond grade three
Later becoming Canada's leading exporter
Of high-quality radio telephones
And accidental founder of a major airline
And one of the best chroniclers of this rainy coast
In both words and paintings

I had my own story to tell of Capt. Vancouver
Ducking through his first Nootka doorpost
And shape-shifting islands hovering over horizons
A tale I hinted at but never got around to
Unfolding in its full oceanic sprawl
Which often gives me a feeling of misspent life

But when I think of that galaxy of voices
I served as the conduit for

And the firmament of followers they called out
Of emptiness, all avowing, "We, too…"
Then I think I should not feel shortchanged
Though I have to force the argument.

TOUGH BUG

The doctrine makers like Yvor Winters
John Crowe Ransom and Charles Olson
Whose hard theorems put one off
Cripple all who would try to follow
And cripple themselves as their
Living matter shrinks down
The sides of their hard container
Still manage to occasionally break free
As in "Bells for John Whiteside's Daughter"
And write some truly moving verse

Which just goes to show
The bacterium of poetic inspiration
Can survive and even thrive
In the most adverse conditions

POETRY

Poetry is one of those things humans do that doesn't make sense
You just have to accept it as an incurable habit, like hoarding.
You will see respectable grandmothers, insurance executives and bums
Parade up to the mike and read this set of words
Nobody in the audience understands, then go sit down
Proud of having done it
People clap, thinking,"I must be taking part in something improving."
And it goes on and on that way for centuries
You'd think it would wither away for lack of purpose
But no, it hangs on like malaria
You see attractive young Asian women busting their butts to be poets.
There is no use asking them why
Or maybe there is: sometimes the sportscaster approach gets a
    surprising result
"Ms. Lam, when you read that last line up there, what did you feel?"
"Well, Bernie, I felt like I had transcended the physical. Hi Mom."
This is a clue then: at some point in their lives
Whether they know it consciously or not
Everybody wants to transcend the physical
Everybody wants to collect the humdrum evidence of their lives
The soiled underwear, the smelly shoes, the sad Mondays
And fire it into incandescence, alchemize it into pure light
Sizzling off toward deep space at 186 thousand miles per second

You can't blame them
So that's the motive, but what still needs explaining
Is how do they find out about it
And why do they approach it from so many different ways
You have the oriental sage chiselling his constipated haiku counting
    syllables

/ 115

Walt Whitman spewing his diarrhetic yawp not even counting pages
You have the flat-footed Tagores and Nerudas and David McFaddens
Leaving you to find the light between the words on your own
Others like Rilke never start until they're already at warp speed
Flying by high overhead, missed by all but the most curious
The lightning bug is undiscerning
I once had to deal with a brain-damaged woman
Who wouldn't stop churning it out
Swamped me with unintelligible manuscripts
You have the bunkhouse balladeers and cowboy poets
Snaggle-toothed illiterates out-doing each other with clever rhymes
Never writing anything down.
Incredibly serious young careerists clog the masters programs
Lamenting that their book sales don't break the 100 mark
Write screeds warning this augurs the end of civilization
Even as the postal system bogs down with more unpublished poems

ACKNOWLEDGEMENTS

These poems are nobody's fault but my own although several folks have given me very sympathetic and palliative counsel. Chief among these is Tom Wayman, a great Canadian poet and tireless encourager of writing impulses of all shapes and sizes. Tom it was who figuratively gathered these ruminations off the floor and assembled them into something that has even me half convinced is a book. If memory serves he performed a similar service for previous books of mine. Tom, your sainthood awaits. Right now I can't think of too many others. Most of my writer friends turn suspiciously silent when I try to bring up the subject of my own so-called verses. A glorious exception would be Lorna Crozier, who has been a fount of encouragement and support down the years, though she has not seen any of these poems. Brian Kaufman and the sturdy crew at Anvil have earned my eternal gratitude by putting themselves on the line for this book, which gives me such confidence in it as I am able to have. My wife Mary wasn't forced to make any extraordinary sacrifices that I can think of other than putting up with me monotonously tapping away during what should have been conjugal morning coffee times, refraining from peeking or asking me what I was up to. She knows I hate that.

Some of these poems have been previously published in *Event, Geist, Cascadia Magazine* and—I think that's it. I'm not a very energetic submitter.

Howard White was born in 1945 in Abbotsford, British Columbia. He was raised in a series of camps and settlements on the BC coast and never got over it. He is still to be found stuck barnacle-like to the shore at Pender Harbour, BC. He started *Raincoast Chronicles* and Harbour Publishing in the early 1970s and some of his other books include *The Men There Were Then*, *The Sunshine Coast*, *Patrick and the Backhoe* and *The Airplane Ride*. His selected works, *Writing in the Rain*, won the Stephen Leacock Medal for Humour. He has also been awarded the Order of BC and the Order of Canada. His previous book of poetry, *Ghost in the Gears*, was a finalist for the Dorothy Livesay Prize.